WOULD YOU RATHER?...

Over **300** CRAZY QUESTIONS!

Supremely STRANGE

Justin Heimberg & David Gomberg

Published by Seven Footer Press
165 Madison Avenue
Suite 201
New York, NY 10016
First Printing, July 2014
10 9 8 7 6 5 4 3 2
Manufactured in Mayfield, Pennsylvania, 07/14
© Copyright Justin Heimberg and David Gomberg, 2014
All Rights Reserved

Would You Rather...?® is a registered trademark used under license from Spin Master Ltd.

Design by Thomas Schirtz

ISBN 978-1-939158-26-0

www.sevenfooterpress.com

CONTENTS

DISCONTENTS

STRANGE THINGS AHEAD!

You are about to enter the wild and wondrous world of
the **SUPREMELY STRANGE.**
(Cue eerie music.)

A world where odd things are common,
and common things are odd.
(Cue more eerie music.)

A world of the unpredictable...
the unmentionable... the unimaginable.
(Tell you what... Let's just keep the eerie music going. Okay?)

Consider the next page a creaking, rusty-hinged door
into a house of hilarious horrors.
(Alright, cut the music. This is overkill.)

Overkill... exactly what will happen to you if you don't watch out
as you traverse these corrosive corridors...
(What?! Come on, that doesn't even make sense!)

Sense? Who has time for sense in the wild, wondrous world
of the **SUPREMELY STRANGE.** Cue eerie music.
*(Wait, I'm in charge of the music! You know what? I don't even care
any more. I'm getting a sandwich. Just cue the eerie music.)*

HOW TO USE THIS BOOK

GAME 1: FREESTYLE

1. Sit around with a bunch of friends.

2. Read a question from the book out loud and talk about it. You won't believe some of the stuff you'll come up with as you think about which choice to make.

3. Everybody must choose! That's the whole point. It forces you to really think about the options.

4. Once everyone has chosen, move on to the next question.

GAME 2: DEBATE

Pick one of the options from a *Would You Rather...?* question and assign the other option to a friend. Argue against each other about which option is better. Have a third person decide who won the debate. Break ties by dance-off.

GAME 3: PREDICTION

Select a question and choose a designated "player."
Everyone predicts what that player will choose and gives
reasons for their predictions. Be nice-ish.

GAME 4: NINJA STRIKE

Find a horde of bandits that is raiding merchant caravans
and marauding towns. Train in the martial arts, specializing
in "book warfare." Tear out the book's pages and fashion
them into folded throwing stars or other pieces of deadly
weaponry. Defeat bandits.

CHAPTER ONE

STRANGE

Would you rather...

have fish hook fingernails

OR

screwdriver toenails?

Would you rather...

every day, have to eat your lunch in two minutes or less

OR

have to brush your teeth for two hours or longer?

YOU MUST CHOOSE!

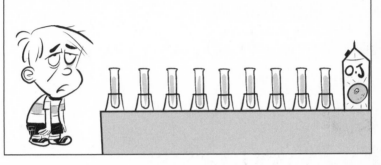

WOULD YOU RATHER...HAVE TO DRINK ALL LIQUIDS FROM TEST TUBES

OR FROM A CRAZY STRAW THAT IS 200 FEET LONG?

Would you rather...

have a cell phone case that magically flies your phone to you whenever you whistle

OR

have school books that magically flutter behind you so that you don't have to carry them?

Would you rather...

use broccoli-flavored lip balm

OR

burnt toast-scented deodorant?

YOU MUST CHOOSE!

Would you rather...

change the first letter of your first name to *P*

OR

to *V*?

Would you rather...

age a full year every day

OR

gain ten pounds every day?

Things to consider: playing soccer, Instagram posts; How long would you survive with each choice?

YOU MUST CHOOSE!

Would you rather...

have a unicorn horn on your forehead **OR** on your chin?

on your knee **OR** on your elbow?

on your right foot **OR** on your left butt-cheek?

Things to consider: impaling yourself when you sneeze (chin); self-defense (knee, elbow); sitting difficulties/advantages (butt)

YOU MUST CHOOSE!

Would you rather...

communicate in a language based on pinching

OR

based on farting?

Things to consider: conversing in a library, heated arguments, soreness

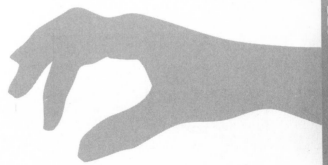

YOU MUST CHOOSE!

WOULD YOU RATHER...HAVE TO ALWAYS RIDE IN THE TRUNK OF A CAR

OR RIDE STRAPPED TO THE ROOF?

Would you rather...

hug the closest person to you every day at 11:42 am

OR

at 8:36 pm?

Would you rather...

be able to silence your footsteps

OR

have an echo that sounds like a full gospel choir?

YOU MUST CHOOSE!

STRANGE

9

Would you rather...

live on the 111ᵗʰ floor with no elevator

OR

live on an island that you had to swim a mile (32 laps) to get to and from? (You can't use a boat.)

Would you rather...

only be able to swim freestyle

OR

stand Gangnam-style?

YOU MUST CHOOSE!

Would you rather...

always have to wear a bloody bandage around your head

OR

always have to wear a thousand Band-Aids somewhere on your body?

Things to consider: explaining what happened; Where would you put the Band-Aids?

Would you rather...

only be able to photograph yourself by taking "selfies"

OR

only be able to have your picture taken by photo-bombing other people's photos?

YOU MUST CHOOSE!

YOU CHOOSE!

Captain America **OR** The Incredible Hulk?

As your lifeguard?

As your tennis doubles partner?

As your accountant?

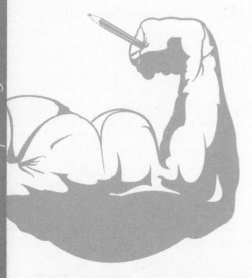

YOU MUST CHOOSE!

ACTION!

Would you rather...

have your only dance be the "Wounded Penguin"

OR

the "Heads or Tails?"
Demonstrate what you think each dance is!

YOU MUST CHOOSE!

13

Would you rather...

whenever you get disappointed, have sad "wha-wha-wha-whaaaa" trombone music play

OR

whenever you get too excited, "tilt" like an old pinball machine and stop working for a while?

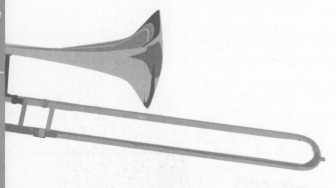

YOU MUST CHOOSE!

WOULD YOU RATHER....HAVE A THUMB-SUCKING HABIT THROUGH YOUR MID-THIRTIES

STOCKS

OR HAVE A THUMB-SUCKING HABIT UNTIL YOU ARE TWELVE YEARS OLD (BUT WITH OTHER PEOPLE'S THUMBS)?

VEGAS OR BUST

CHAPTER TWO

2

GETTING SCHOOLED

Would you rather...

have your book reports graded like on *The Voice* where teachers turn around if they like what they hear

OR

have your reports graded by school vote like on *American Idol*?

Would you rather...

have your school principal be Poseidon **OR** Zeus?

Vladimir Putin **OR** Darth Vader?

your dad **OR** your mom?

YOU MUST CHOOSE!

WOULD YOU RATHER....HAVE A NINJA FOR A SCHOOL JANITOR

OR A SAMURAI CROSSING GUARD?

Would you rather play this book with...

your Science teacher **OR** your English teacher?

your Math teacher **OR** your Social Studies/History teacher?

your Art teacher **OR** Gym teacher?

YOU MUST CHOOSE!

Would you rather have the school water fountains filled with...

orange soda **OR** hot caramel?

Gatorade **OR** pudding?

water that barely dribbles out of the spout **OR**
water that shoots out with the pressure of a fire hose?

YOU MUST CHOOSE!

Would you rather...

have a magic pencil that always writes the correct answer

OR

a magic marker that can write in the air?

Would you rather...

have to walk to and from school in the snow, uphill (both ways) for a mile each way

OR

at the day's final school bell, have a bull released (like in the Running of the Bulls in Pamplona, Spain) as you try to flee through the halls?

Follow up: Would you try to save yourself or help other people?

YOU MUST CHOOSE!

22

Would you rather your school have...

no chairs **OR** no tables?

no math **OR** no reading?

no teachers **OR** no gravity?

Things to consider: lunch, P.E., Art class

YOU MUST CHOOSE!

WOULD YOU RATHER... COMPULSIVELY RAISE YOUR HAND FOR EVERY QUESTION IN CLASS EVEN IF YOU DON'T KNOW THE ANSWER

WHAT WAS THE CAUSE OF THE REFORMS UNDERTAKEN BY MUSTAFA KEMAL ATATURK DURING HIS RULE IN TURKEY?

GULP!

OR ANSWER EVERY 8TH QUESTION ON ANY TEST: "TULSA, OKLAHOMA?"

NAME BILLY
#8
9 X 7 = ?
ANS: TULSA, OKLAH

Would you rather...

have Benihana-style cafeteria tables and cooks in your school cafeteria

OR

have *Hunger Games*-like training zones on your school playground?

Would you rather...

go to a school where the school uniform code requires students to dress up as a superhero

OR

as a character from *Lord of the Rings*?

Follow up: Who would you choose to dress up as?

YOU MUST CHOOSE!

BEST OF!

Pick one of the following:

Cosmos' host Neil deGrasse Tyson as your science teacher?

World Wrestling Entertainment's Brock Lesnar as your gym teacher?

Marvel's Black Widow as your school nurse?

Diary of a Wimpy Kid author Jeff Kinney as your art teacher?

Star Wars' Obi-Wan Kenobi as your guidance counselor?

YOU MUST CHOOSE!

Would you rather...

have a P.E. unit in trapeze-flying

OR

paintball?

Would you rather have to read everything...

IN THIS FONT **OR** ~~in this font~~ ?

this font **OR** this font?

 **OR** ?

YOU MUST CHOOSE!

Would you rather...

your school was decorated with disco balls and lights

OR

with Fathead wall decals of you in action?

YOU MUST CHOOSE!

ACTION!

Would you rather...

if your life depended on it, using only your head, solve a math problem

OR

answer a geography question?

Test your choice:

Option 1: 11x15 = ?

Option 2: What is the capital of South Korea?[1]

YOU MUST CHOOSE!

Would you rather...

present all school reports in battle rap

OR

by puppet show?

Would you rather...

have the *FOX NFL Sunday* guys show up half-way through the school day with highlights, commenting on how your day has gone

OR

have an intense NFL coach show up, yell at you, and give you a pep talk to finish your day?

YOU MUST CHOOSE!

Would you rather...

have a strange disorder where every time you hear a whistle, you play dead like a possum for an hour

OR

where every time you hear a school bell, you think you are a World War II submarine captain on active duty?

Would you rather...

replace your desk chair with a unicycle

OR

replace your desk with a tethered goat?

YOU MUST CHOOSE!

Would you rather...

have your school morning announcements read by shock jock DJs

OR

by excitable soccer announcers as if they were calling a game?

YOU MUST CHOOSE!

If a magic spell turned your school supplies
into evil, living creatures, would you rather battle...

a stapler **OR** a staple remover?

a bunch of binder clips **OR** rubber bands?

a hole-puncher **OR** a label maker?

a bag of red rubber balls **OR** the copier?

YOU MUST CHOOSE!

CHAPTER THREE

GROSSLY UNPLEASANT
AND UNPLEASANTLY GROSS

Would you rather...

get peanut butter caught in your hair

OR

get hair caught in your peanut butter?

Things to consider: really bad candy bar idea

Would you rather...

after eating an oatmeal cookie, learn that the raisins were actually dead flies

OR

wolf down a sundae only to learn that the whipped cream was frothed-up dog slobber?

YOU MUST CHOOSE!

WOULD YOU RATHER...BE ABLE TO BATHE/SHOWER USING ONLY YOUR TOILET

OR ONLY BE ABLE TO USE YOUR TOASTER FOR HEAT?

Would you rather...

kiss a coyote on the snout

OR

kiss a leaf of poison ivy?

Would you rather...

have birdseed dandruff

OR

poppy seed pimples?

Things to consider: going to the beach, scabs from being picked at/pecked at

YOU MUST CHOOSE!

DRINK UP!

Would you rather...

only be able to drink from puddles **OR** from used sponges?

from sprinklers **OR** from gutter spouts?

from aquariums **OR** only be able to go the bathroom in them?

YOU MUST CHOOSE!

Would you rather...

drink milk that was left out of the fridge for a week

OR

milk straight from a cow's udder?

YOU MUST CHOOSE!

Would you rather...

squeeze the blood out of a bloated leech and dip your French fries in it

OR

spread a bird's freshly regurgitated breakfast on your English Muffin and eat it?

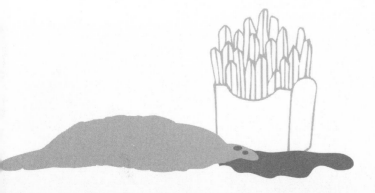

YOU MUST CHOOSE!

Would you rather...

be limited to 100 steps a day

OR

100 words a day?

Follow up: How would you use your steps? Would you need a ride to school? Would you piggyback to class? How would you choose/use your 100 words? Would you learn sign language?

YOU MUST CHOOSE!

ALL OR NOTHING!

Would you rather...

never be able to eat dessert **OR** only be able to eat dessert?

never be able to watch cartoons **OR** only be able to watch cartoons?

never be able to dance **OR** always be dancing?

YOU MUST CHOOSE!

Would you rather...

not be able to turn on any lights in your home for a month

OR

not be allowed to flush any toilets in your home for a month?

YOU MUST CHOOSE!

Would you rather only be able to clean yourself...

with used squeegees from gas stations

OR

by using Old Faithful?

...and then dry off with...

only toilet paper

OR

sandpaper?

YOU MUST CHOOSE!

45

WHAT SNOT TO LOVE?

Which would you rather have as snot?

grape soda **OR** Play-Doh?

hair gel **OR** maple syrup?

Crazy String **OR** Krazy Glue?

Things to consider: sneezing, breakfast, allergy season, blowing your nose right onto your tongue

YOU MUST CHOOSE!

WOULD YOU RATHER...HAVE YOUR NOSE ROTATED 90 DEGREES

ATCHOO!

OR HAVE TEETH THAT LOOK LIKE THE STALAGMITES AND STALACTITES OF A CAVE?

YOU MUST CHOOSE!

Would you rather...

on school picture day,

get a black eye **OR** break out in a dozen big zits?

have a bad cold **OR** a bad case of pink eye?

lose three front teeth **OR** gain three?

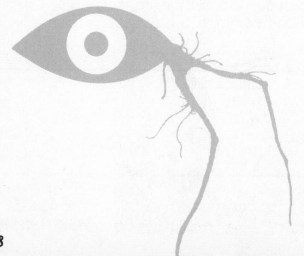

YOU MUST CHOOSE!

Would you rather...

eat a bowl of "mac & cheese" made up of ribbed, slimy, wriggling earthworms tossed in thick, gooey, green caterpillar-guts

OR

eat a "hot dog" made of Goliath Beetle larvae?

YOU MUST CHOOSE!

Would you rather...

on a hundred degree day, eat a tuna salad ice cream cone

OR

use a stick of butter for deodorant?

YOU MUST CHOOSE!

YOU CHOOSE!

Ear, Nose **OR** Throat?

Get a gnat stuck in?

Get completely clogged?

Have three of?

YOU MUST CHOOSE!

Would you rather...

"snart" (sneeze and fart at the same time)

OR

"vurp" (vomit a little when you burp)?

Accidental Education: When you combine words together like in the question above, it's called a "portmanteau" (pronounced port-man-toe) word, which is French for a suitcase that opens into two parts. Popular portmanteaus include brunch (breakfast + lunch) and smog (smoke + fog). Sorry for the learning!

YOU MUST CHOOSE!

Would you rather...

in an instant, have every freckle on your body turn into a tick

OR

have your saliva turn into extra-extra-extra-spicy hot sauce?

Would you rather...

have all your shirts made from flypaper

OR

all your pants made from plastic wrap?

Things to consider: starting a trend, running

YOU MUST CHOOSE!

WOULD YOU RATHER....USE A MELON BALLER TO DIG A 1000 FOOT DITCH

OR USE TWEEZERS TO PLUCK ALL THE GRASS ON A SOCCER FIELD?

Would you rather...

get noogied by a rubber fist attached to a power drill

OR

get wedgied by a construction crane?

YOU MUST CHOOSE!

Would you rather...

get tossed in a giant Caesar salad

OR

get shaken up in a giant Boggle word cube pen?

Things to consider: crouton bruises, vowel movements

Would you rather...

have cold sores

OR

warm sores?

YOU MUST CHOOSE!

Would you rather...

have sneezes that sound like a laser gun firing

OR

farts that sound like Rihanna?

YOU MUST CHOOSE!

NAVEL STATION

Would you rather...

have a six-inch-long outie belly button

OR

an innie that goes through your whole body, clear through your back?

Would you rather...

have an alien creature living in your belly button

OR

have a literal belly "button" that keeps your insides in unless it becomes unfastened?

YOU MUST CHOOSE!

Would you rather...

for the rest of your life, use the same towel **OR** the same socks? (No washing.)

the same napkin **OR** the same Kleenex?

the same Band-Aid **OR** the same piece of toilet paper?

YOU MUST CHOOSE!

CHAPTER FOUR

GOOD SPORTS, BAD SPORTS

Would you rather...

always throw a strike in baseball

OR

always throw a strike in bowling?
Things to consider: Which one would lead to more money? More fun?
What would you do with your skills?

Would you rather...

without any training, ski jump

OR

cliff-dive?

YOU MUST CHOOSE!

WOULD YOU RATHER SEE...AS AN OLYMPIC SPORT, A COMBINATION OF POLE-VAULTING AND ARCHERY

OR HURDLES AND SUDOKU?

Would you rather...

have your favorite professional basketball team change its team name to your last name (for example, "The Washington Grunspans")

OR

have your face painted on the side of your favorite professional football team's helmet?

YOU MUST CHOOSE!

HOW BIG OF A WIMP ARE YOU?

Would you rather...

get hit by a pitch **OR** strike out at the plate?

run out of bounds **OR** get tackled after gaining just one more yard?

be an ultimate fighter **OR** ultimate flee-er (where you have perfected over 1,000 ways to run away)?

YOU MUST CHOOSE!

RULE CHANGE!

Would you rather...

change the NFL rules so that fans are allowed to make one tackle per game

OR

change Major League Baseball so that the ball explodes at a random time once a game?

YOU MUST CHOOSE!

Would you rather...

only be able to exercise in a giant hamster wheel

OR

in a giant hamster ball?

Would you rather...

never be able to watch sports

OR

never be able to play them?

YOU MUST CHOOSE!

Would you rather...

wrestle a 300-pound 70-year-old

OR

a 100-pound 30-year-old?

Would you rather...

if you win a big game, have Gatorade poured over your head

OR

not?

YOU MUST CHOOSE!

For a touchdown celebration, would you rather...

do the "Buddha" where you sit cross-legged and meditate **OR** the "Gardener" where you mime like you are lawn-mowing the end zone and weed-whack around the goal post?

the "Plastic Bag" where you roll around on the grass aimlessly **OR** the "Ballerina" where you daintily twirl across the end zone?

the "Drying Pelt" where you climb the goal post and hang limply over it **OR** the "Picker" where you lazily grab clumps of grass and stuff them into your pants?

YOU MUST CHOOSE!

WOULD YOU RATHER...CELEBRATE YOUR TOUCHDOWNS WITH "THE BABY" WHERE YOU SOB, SPIT-UP, AND TAKE A NAP

OR WITH THE "THE WOODPECKER" WHERE YOU SMASH YOUR HEAD AGAINST GOAL POST REPEATEDLY?

Would you rather...

play a sport called Air Football where all the players have jetpacks

OR

be in a "fantasy" football league where all the players have powers like wizards?

Follow up: What plays would you draw up for Air Football? What powers would you use in what way on your "fantasy" team?

YOU MUST CHOOSE!

Would you rather...

be unable to stop swinging your hips as if you're swinging a hula hoop

OR

be unable to stop swinging your arm as if you're throwing a Frisbee?

Things to consider: baseball at-bats, job interviews, muscle growth

YOU MUST CHOOSE!

EXTREME SPORTS!

Would you rather...

watch Bar-on-Fire High Jump **OR** Vertical Javelin?

Quicksand Long Jump **OR** Alligator Pit Triple Jump?

Dry-Ice Hockey (where players must play shirtless and in shorts) **OR** Figure Skating with a Zamboni Death Vehicle™ on the loose?

YOU MUST CHOOSE!

Would you rather...

have Dick Vitale do commentary for all of your basketball games

OR

have your soccer games called by that Spanish language soccer announcer who yells "Goaaaalllllllll!"?

Would you rather...

play against LeBron James in Four Square

OR

play against Albert Pujols in Tee Ball?

YOU MUST CHOOSE!

ACTION!

Would you rather...

with a bet at stake, try to do 20 sit-ups in a row

OR

answer three history trivia questions?

Try your choice!

Who was the third president?

Who started the Underground Railroad?

Which one of the following is not a historical event: The Missouri Compromise, The Louisiana Purchase, or the St. Louis Blues?

Answers: Thomas Jefferson, Harriet Tubman the St. Louis Blues

YOU MUST CHOOSE!

Better Super Bowl Half-Time Show?

a Civil War Reenactment **OR** a supermodel pie-eating contest?

a musical tribute to you and your best friends by One Direction **OR** a boy band of overweight offensive linemen?

a T-shirt cannon fight **OR** magician David Blaine revealing the final score written under every attendee's seat cushion?

YOU MUST CHOOSE!

WOULD YOU RATHER....ALWAYS HAVE TO WEAR HOCKEY SKATES

OR A HOCKEY MASK?

CHAPTER FIVE

PIZZA POSSIBILITIES AND OTHER FANTASTICAL FOODSTUFFS

Would you rather...

eat pizza with ants crawling all over it

OR

eat pizza with mashed-caterpillar-gut pesto sauce?

Would you rather...

eat a bowl of Froot Loops in a gravity-free chamber

OR

eat a rack of barbecue ribs while skydiving?

Follow up: Which would take longer? What would be your plan for both? Which would be messier? Which would make you throw up? And if you did in either case, what would happen then?

YOU MUST CHOOSE!

WOULD YOU RATHER....EAT LUNCH OUT OF TROUGHS LIKE BARN ANIMALS

OR HAVE TO HUNT AND PREPARE YOUR OWN FOOD AT LUNCH?

NEW DIET FADS

Need to lose weight? Here are some out-of-the-box ideas. Let's move!

Would you rather...

only be able to eat green foods

OR

only be able to eat foods that start with the letter "c"?

Things to consider: salad, corn, green candy, chowder, cucumber, curly fries, curly-everything, green food coloring

Would you rather...

only eat food that is still growing on something

OR

only eat food left on other people's plates at restaurants?

YOU MUST CHOOSE!

Would you rather have to eat all your meals with...

one chopstick **OR** three chopsticks?

a math compass **OR** a stapler?

your hands **OR** German Chancellor Angela Merkel?

Would you rather...

have all food stuck in a hard-to-open oyster shell

OR

have to solve a gnome's riddle before being allowed to sit at the table for a meal?

YOU MUST CHOOSE!

Would you rather...

eat the pizza crust bits

OR

just leave them?

Would you rather...

all your food be as hot as just-boiled tea

OR

always be ice-cold?

YOU MUST CHOOSE!

Would you rather have your pizza delivered by...

secret agents **OR** unmanned drones?

pizza pie-hurling clowns **OR** zombies?

catapults **OR** Bob the Builder?

CIA PIZZA

YOU MUST CHOOSE!

Would you rather...

be capable of toasting bread by breathing on it

OR

be able to scramble eggs with your mind?
Things to consider: work at a restaurant, Jedi Knight possibilities
(well, maybe back-up Jedi Knight)

Would you rather...

use a used Kleenex as a napkin

OR

use a hospital bed pan to cook up a stack of pancakes?

YOU MUST CHOOSE!

Would you rather...

live in a world where it rained spaghetti

OR

where it hailed jelly-filled doughnut holes?
Things to consider: windshield-wiping, getting hit, cleanup; What type of pasta would you prefer it to rain?

Would you rather...

take a bath in chocolate Magic Shell and then have to eat yourself clean

OR

not?

YOU MUST CHOOSE!

Would you rather...

for a minute, chew on a regurgitated cow cud

OR

a slug?

Accidental Education: A "cud" is a piece of food that an animal regurgitates from its stomach to its mouth to be chewed for a second time. The process of rechewing the cud to further break down plant matter and help digestion is called "rumination."

Even More Accidental Education: When we consider something in our minds, we "ruminate" about it, "chewing on" and "turning over" our thoughts. (Again, we sincerely apologize for the learning.)

YOU MUST CHOOSE!

Would you rather...

immediately put anything given to you in your mouth like a baby

OR

have to be burped after each meal by your mom like a baby?

Things to ruminate on: getting tests back in school, eating out at restaurants

YOU MUST CHOOSE!

WOULD YOU RATHER...BE A SUPER HERO CALLED "PIZZA MAN" WHO TWIRLED AND THREW DOUGH AT BAD GUYS

OR BE A SUPER HERO CALLED "THE BELLBOY" WHO WAS SKILLED AT COMBAT USING LUGGAGE?

Would you rather...

be tarred and feathered

OR

caramelled and nutted?

Things to consider: birds, bugs, using it as armor

YOU MUST CHOOSE!

DISGUSTING DIGESTING:

Would you rather...

gargle with olive juice

OR

brush your teeth with hot pepper toothpaste?

Would you rather...

eat a soap-congealed drain-clog hairburger

OR

eat a link of earwax sausage stuffed in shedded snake skin?

YOU MUST CHOOSE!

Worse Pizza Topping!

moss **OR** toenail clippings?

roadkill kabob **OR** poison ivy?

larva **OR** lava?

Would you rather...

chew a pack of asparagus-flavored gum

OR

suck on a roll of assorted fish-flavored Life-Savers?

YOU MUST CHOOSE!

POWERS, FANTASIES, AND OTHER GOOD THINGS

Would you rather...

be able to jump/dive into water with no splash

OR

be able to make a splash as big as a grand piano dropping into the water from 100 feet?

Things to consider: Olympic diving career, splashing lifeguards, pond drainage business

Would you rather...

be a deadly assassin who uses playing cards

OR

Super Balls?

YOU MUST CHOOSE!

Would you rather...

have a shower that keeps you clean for a month

OR

have a bed that gives you a full-night's sleep in one hour?

YOU MUST CHOOSE!

Would you rather...

have complimentary front row tickets to every concert

OR

every sporting event?

Follow up: What would be the top five things you would see? What sign would you bring? What would you yell as a fan/heckler?

YOU MUST CHOOSE!

Would you rather have on your battle-rap team...

Eminem

OR

Shakespeare?

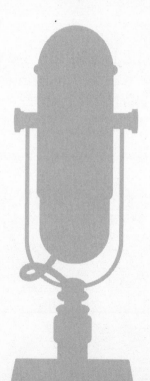

YOU MUST CHOOSE!

Would you rather have as a pet...

a fat cat **OR** small dog?

a living snowman like Olaf in *Frozen* **OR** a *Despicable Me* minion?

a living blanket that told you bedtime stories **OR** a living piano that played music to fit your mood?

a goose that lays golden eggs **OR** a platypus that lays rare Pokémons?

a miniature pony **OR** a giant hamster?

YOU MUST CHOOSE!

Would you rather...

own a TV with every movie on it

OR

own an iPad with every app in the iTunes store?

Would you rather...

live in a house that's self-cleaning

OR

have a car that's self-driving?

YOU MUST CHOOSE!

Would you rather...

have a force field around you that magically keeps bugs away

OR

that keeps annoying people away?

Would you rather...

know exactly what the weather will be each day as soon as you wake up

OR

be able to magically fit into any article of clothing?

YOU MUST CHOOSE!

Would you rather...

if offered, tattoo every inch of your face for 15 million dollars

OR

decline the offer?

Things to consider: You can get the tattoos removed, but just know that tattoo removal is ten times more painful than getting one. Something to think about later in life 😊

YOU MUST CHOOSE!

Would you rather...

be Facebook friends with every single person on Facebook but have no in-person friends

OR

have five actual good real-life friends but no online friends?

Would you rather...

have the power to see with your eyes closed

OR

have a second mouth on the back of your neck capable of independent conversation?

YOU MUST CHOOSE!

Would you rather...

be a vampire **OR** a wizard?

an elf **OR** a dwarf?

a werewolf **OR** a were-Charles Barkley?

YOU MUST CHOOSE!

FACT VS. FICTION!

Choose between the following items from mythology and real world items!

Would you rather...

have Hermes' winged sandals **OR** the Hope Diamond (valued at $2,000,000)?

Harry Potter's Nimbus 2000 flying broomstick **OR** your own private jet?

a light saber **OR** a Buick LaSabre?

YOU MUST CHOOSE!

FACTUAL FICTION VS. FICTIONAL FICTION!

Choose between the following famous mythological items and items from mythologies we just made up!

Would you rather...

have *Mjölnir*, Thor's magic hammer **OR** *Jjorblik*, a magical box from Ikea that assembles anything placed into it?

Poseidon's Trident (creates thunderstorms and tidal waves) **OR** Poseidon's lesser-known Spork (creates stains on people's clothing)?

Hades' helm of invisibility **OR** a hat that instantly perfectly styles your hair?

YOU MUST CHOOSE!

109

Would you rather...

have Bill Gates leave his entire fortune to you

OR

live for 200 years?

Would you rather...

live in a world where humans have ram horns on our heads

OR

on our butts?

Things to consider: ramming battles, being our own rocking chairs

YOU MUST CHOOSE!

Would you rather...

get to spend a week in outer space

OR

a week in the White House?

Would you rather...

be able to make balloon animals that come to life and follow your every command

OR

paper origami creatures that come to life?

YOU MUST CHOOSE!

111

Would you rather...

be able to juggle

OR

be able to dunk any object other than a basketball?

YOU MUST CHOOSE!

ANIMAL ADAPTATIONS

Would you rather...

have porcupine quills for nose hairs that shoot out when you sneeze

OR

be able to spit with enough power and accuracy to knock down prey from trees?

Accidental education: There is a type of fish known as the Archer Fish that does precisely the second option. Its mouth is specially designed to shoot water like a squirt gun and its eyes have evolved to allow it to see through water into the air so it can shoot down bugs from overhanging branches.

YOU MUST CHOOSE!

113

Would you rather...

receive in the mail one of every product you see advertised on TV (you get it the next day)

OR

have the ability to read the future in snot patterns blown in tissues?

YOU MUST CHOOSE!

Would you rather be able to move with your mind...

bricks **OR** pies?

bats (baseball) **OR** bats (animal)?

things that rhyme with "lick" **OR** with "loose?"

YOU MUST CHOOSE!

WOULD YOU RATHER....RECEIVE $1000 A MONTH IN ADVERTISING DOLLARS BY PERMANENTLY WEARING CONTACTS OF DIFFERENT CORPORATE LOGOS

OR BY GETTING TATTOOS OF DIFFERENT LOGOS?

With LEGO, would you rather...

build what the instructions say

OR

build something from your imagination?

Would you rather...

have detachable throwing star earrings

OR

nunchuck bracelets?

YOU MUST CHOOSE!

CHAPTER SEVEN

SUPREMELY STRANGE

WOULD YOU RATHER...ONLY BE ABLE TO MOVE AROUND BY CRAWLING

OR ONLY BE ABLE TO EAT THINGS THAT ARE ALIVE?

Would you rather...

battle a rabbit the size of a rhino

OR

a rhino the size of a rabbit?

Would you rather...

have to write with your bad hand

OR

have to play sports with your bad hand?

YOU MUST CHOOSE!

Which would you rather say at three random times every day?

"Fire!" **OR** "Silence!"?

"What is that?" **OR** "Happy Birthday!"?

"I love you!" (romantic) **OR** "Gimme five!" (romantic)?

five seconds of loud, raucous laughter **OR** five seconds of heavy, racking sobs?

"Bonzai!" **OR** "The overlord shall be pleased."?

Things to consider: Think of some different times over the past few days and think about what would have happened if you said any of the phrases above.

YOU MUST CHOOSE!

Would you rather...

etirw sdrawkcab

OR

kaeps sdrawkcab?

Would you rather...

always have to wear flip flops

OR

super-warm winter boots?

YOU MUST CHOOSE!

Would you rather...

instead of fingers, have five tongues on your hand

OR

have five permanently lit candles?
Things to consider: birthday cake, shaking hands to greet someone, mailing letters

Would you rather...

have Mr. Spock's ears

OR

his eyebrows?
Things to consider: hats, headbands, looking concerned

YOU MUST CHOOSE!

Would you rather...

have detachable antlers

OR

a retractable monkey tail?

Would you rather...

go to the bathroom once every five minutes

OR

once every five years, but have it take three months to relieve yourself?

YOU MUST CHOOSE!

Would you rather...

be a conjoined twin connected by a shared beard

OR

by a shared fingernail?

Things to consider: growing over time (you, the beard, the nail), people jumping rope over the beard, dancing

Would you rather...

whenever you get an A on a test, be doused with Gatorade by your classmates

OR

whenever you get a C or lower, be forced to write your grade in red paint on your forehead and be unable to wash it until the next morning?

YOU MUST CHOOSE!

Would you rather...

be dumped on by a garbage truck for five minutes

OR

by a cement truck for ten seconds?

YOU MUST CHOOSE!

Would you rather...

lick an elephant

OR

get licked by an elephant?

a fox?

a certified public accountant?

Would you rather...

have to cut your own hair

OR

have to make your own clothes?

YOU MUST CHOOSE!

For the rest of your life, would you rather only be able to drive...

a tractor **OR** an old motorcycle?

a horse-drawn carriage **OR** a post-apocalyptic dune buggy?

a Mars rover **OR** a motorized dessert cart?

YOU MUST CHOOSE!

Would you rather...

only be able to communicate with charades

OR

with an Etch-A-Sketch?

Would you rather...

never be allowed to wear a seatbelt

OR

socks?

YOU MUST CHOOSE!

Would you rather...

always choose the second option no matter what is asked

OR

always choose the first option?

Things to consider: If I choose the second option of this question, then I have to choose the first option which means I have to choose the second option... Does not compute!... But then the second option says I must choose the first option... Does not compute!... Overload!... Overloooooooaaaaadddddd.... (Fall to ground.)

YOU MUST CHOOSE!

Would you rather...

wear braces for the rest of your life

OR

a tennis headband with matching wristbands?

Would you rather...

grow hair on your palms

OR

on the inside of your mouth?

YOU MUST CHOOSE!

YOU HAVE BEEN HYPNOTIZED.
Which of the following would you choose?

Whenever someone says "goodbye," you think you are a Spanish conquistador in the middle of a duel

OR

whenever you hear the word "4," you think that the person who's talking to you is an opposing sumo wrestler?

Whenever the clock strikes noon, you think that your clothes are creatures trying to smother you

OR

whenever the clock strikes 3pm, you become utterly convinced that you're a hockey goalie who needs to do everything in your power to prevent anybody and anything from getting past you?

YOU MUST CHOOSE!

Would you rather...

be suddenly magically teleported to a random spot 5,000 miles from where you are right now

OR

to the same spot 500 years from now?

Would you rather...

have a well-attended wedding

OR

a well-attended funeral?

YOU MUST CHOOSE!

YOU CHOOSE!

Katniss Everdeen **OR** Hermione Granger?

Share a locker with?

As your big sister?

On your Kick The Can team?

YOU MUST CHOOSE!

Would you rather...

have half of your entire body weight contained in your feet

OR

in your hands?

Things to consider: walking, boxing, kickball

YOU MUST CHOOSE!

Would you rather...

only be able to use your feet when typing

OR

only be able to use vowels?
Things to consider: Aieeeee!, foot-cramping, EIEIO.

Would you rather...

all your clothing be annoyingly moist

OR

ice-cold?

YOU MUST CHOOSE!

Would you rather...

have a paralyzing fear of sitting **OR** of your reflection?

of bread **OR** babies?

of the color yellow **OR** the letter M?

YOU MUST CHOOSE!

CHAPTER EIGHT

VIDEO GAMES, TOYS AND TECHNOLOGY (AND MAYBE JUST A LITTLE SCIENCE)

Would you rather...

be trapped in a video game

OR

never be able to play them again?

Follow up: Which game would you want to be trapped in? Who would you take with you into the game if you could choose three people? What game would you least like to be trapped in and why?

YOU MUST CHOOSE!

WOULD YOU RATHER....BE AN ENDLESS RUNNER (LIKE IN TEMPLE RUN) WHERE YOU CAN NEVER STOP RUNNING

OR BE AN ENDLESS FARTER (VIDEO GAME YET TO BE CREATED)?

Would you rather...

have an alarm clock that's connected to your home's sprinkler system

OR

an alarm that causes your bed to buck like a bronco?
Things to consider: padding your room, waterproof blankets

YOU MUST CHOOSE!

Would you rather...

never be able to watch your home videos

OR

only be able to watch your home videos and nothing else?

Would you rather...

have a LEGO set based on you and your life

OR

have a video game based on your life?

YOU MUST CHOOSE!

Would you rather...

have motion-activated blinking (you blink whenever something is wiped in front of your face)

OR

have motion-activated yawning?

Things to consider: mosquitos, playing catch, windshield wipers

Would you rather...

have a perfect clone of yourself that will follow all of your orders

OR

have perfect clones of your parents that will follow your orders?

Things to consider: having your double sit in boring classes, parent-teacher conferences

YOU MUST CHOOSE!

Would you rather...

own every video game in the world but have them converted to 8-bit style graphics circa 1986

OR

own only five video games of your choice with their normal graphics?

YOU MUST CHOOSE!

Would you rather...

use a PC **OR** an iPad?

an iPad **OR** Google Glass?

Google Glass **OR** the not-yet-invented
Google Contact Lens?

YOU MUST CHOOSE!

Would you rather...

use hidden cameras to spy on your fellow students

OR

on your teachers?

YOU MUST CHOOSE!

IN THE NAME OF SCIENCE!

Would you rather...

as a zoologist, genetically engineer living slippers that crawl onto your feet when you need them

OR

a living scarf-bird that wraps around you when it's cold?

Would you rather...

as a renegade botanist, genetically engineer a cactus that shoots thorns

OR

glow-in-the-dark flowers?

YOU MUST CHOOSE!

Would you rather...

have a secret cream that made zits disappear

OR

that made them appear?

Things to consider: making yourself look good, making others look bad, creating zit constellation patterns

YOU MUST CHOOSE!

Would you rather...

have a *Disney Infinity* character based on you

OR

a new Avenger based on you?

Would you rather...

when going the bathroom, have a 24 second "shot clock" before your toilet ejects you into the air

OR

have the audio in your bathroom monitored by the government?

YOU MUST CHOOSE!

INVENTOIDS: THE WORLD'S DUMBEST INVENTIONS

Would you rather...

have a "shanger" (a shirt with its own hanger)

OR

"clockets" (clear pockets through which you can read your cell phone)?

YOU MUST CHOOSE!

SURGICAL ENHANCEMENTS

Would you rather...

get a tinted visor surgically inserted into your forehead that can come out with a switch

OR

have wires run through your body so your palms can charge cell phones?

YOU MUST CHOOSE!

WOULD YOU RATHER...LEAVE DARK FINGERPRINTS ON WHATEVER YOU TOUCH

OR LEAVE BLACK GRILL MARKS WHEREVER YOU SIT?

Would you rather...

have a Google Maps add-on that allows you to automatically find missing animals

OR

missing remote controls?

YOU MUST CHOOSE!

Would you rather...

have your entire music collection consist of patriotic songs **OR** preschool songs?

Heavy Metal **OR** smooth jazz?

your relatives singing **OR** llama grunts?

Would you rather...

have your brother or sister edit all your Facebook posts

OR

have Dirk Nowitski photobomb every picture you take?

Things to consider: school pictures, sibling rivalries, wedding portraits

YOU MUST CHOOSE!

Would you rather...

be trapped on a giant foosball table

OR

on a giant air hockey table?

YOU MUST CHOOSE!

CHAPTER NINE

BLANK CHECK

It's time to be part of the creation. Fill in the blanks to discover how hilarious a jokester you can be! The best part is you can play these questions over and over. So you can feel good about saving paper and being environmentally responsible.

Would you rather...

have _____ nostrils
(number)

OR

have four _____s?
(body part)

Would you rather...

be able to fight like a ninja with _____s
(toy)

OR

_____?
(food)

YOU MUST CHOOSE!

Would you rather...

cry _____
(liquid)

OR

sweat _____?
(another liquid)

YOU MUST CHOOSE!

Would you rather...

be roommates with _____
(super hero)

OR

_____?
(video game character)

Would you rather...

change your first name to _____
(random word)

OR

change your last name to _____?
(silly made-up word)

YOU MUST CHOOSE!

Would you rather...

have fingernails made of _____
(type of candy)

OR

have saliva that tastes like _____?
(beverage)

YOU MUST CHOOSE!

Would you rather...

sneeze out of your _____
(body part)

OR

fart out of your _____?
(another body part)

YOU MUST CHOOSE!

Would you rather...

have _____ as your teacher
(Star Trek character)

OR

_____ as your workout partner?
(Star Wars character)

Would you rather...

be stranded on a desert island with _____
(a tool)

OR

with _____?
(celebrity)

YOU MUST CHOOSE!

Would you rather...

have _____ teeth
(number)

OR

_____ fingers?
(number)

YOU MUST CHOOSE!

Would you rather...

live in a world where it snowed _____
                                        (food)

OR

where it rained _____?
                          (soda)

YOU MUST CHOOSE!

BLANK CHECK

Would you rather...

have _____ eyes
              (color)

OR

a _____ tongue?
      (another color)

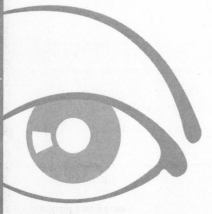

YOU MUST CHOOSE!

Would you rather...

wear clothes made entirely of _____
(material)

OR

never be able to wear _____s?
(piece of clothing)

Would you rather...

be a super villain called Captain _____
(noun)

OR

known as "The _____?"
(Occupation)

YOU MUST CHOOSE!

Would you rather...

be able to fly but only like _____
(strike a pose)

OR

by able to run at near Olympic speed, but like

_____?
(show funny walk)

Would you rather...

eat a 15-month-old _____
(fruit)

OR

ten live _____s?
(insect)

YOU MUST CHOOSE!

Would you rather...

your parents were _____s

(type of monster)

OR

_____s?

(mythological creature)

YOU MUST CHOOSE!

173

Would you rather...

be a Transformer who can change into a _____
(tool)

OR

a _____?
(appliance)

YOU MUST CHOOSE!

Would you rather...

hang out exclusively with people age _____

OR

_____?

Would you rather...

have _____ poops

OR

have _____-scented poops?

YOU MUST CHOOSE!

BLANK CHECK

Would you rather...

have your face look permanently look like _____
(make a face)

OR

like _____?
(make another face)

Would you rather...

have _____ phlegm
(dessert)

OR

have _____ boogers?
(candy)

YOU MUST CHOOSE!

Would you rather...

have a habit of sucking your _____
(body part)

OR

need to always hold a security _____ for comfort?
(object)

YOU MUST CHOOSE!

Would you rather...

be ordered to be in a duel by _____
(weapon)

OR

_____?
(kitchen item)

YOU MUST CHOOSE!

Would you rather...

battle a _____ the size of an elephant
(cute animal)

OR

two _____s the size of a cat?
(wild animal)

YOU MUST CHOOSE!

CHAPTER TEN

WOULD YOU...

Would you... for $10,000, put a leech on your...

Foot?

Stomach?

Forehead?

Follow up: What if you had to keep it there for ten seconds? 30 seconds? Ten minutes?

YOU MUST CHOOSE!

Would you... pick your best friend's nose for a week for an extra ten days vacation from school?

YOU MUST CHOOSE!

Would you... take Justin Bieber's money but have to also take his current state of mind?

YOU MUST CHOOSE!

HOW MUCH?
How much would you pay...

to never get homework?

for a personal butler?

for a personal bodyguard?

for a personal note-taker?

to see a movie trailer of your future?

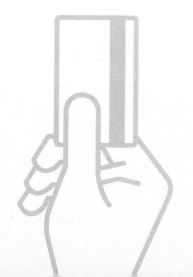

YOU MUST CHOOSE!

WHAT'S YOUR POISON?

Would you... use four squirts of poison ivy nasal spray for $5,000?

Would you... rinse with poison ivy mouthwash for $10,000?

Would you... drink poison ivy tea for $15,000?

Would you... use two-ply poison ivy toilet paper for $20,000?

YOU MUST CHOOSE!

Would you... wear your underwear on the outside of your clothing daily for a week to quadruple that week's allowance?

Follow up: How many weeks would you do it for?

Would you... stick your face into a tank filled with roaches for three minutes for a free trip anywhere in the USA?

Follow up: Where would you choose?

YOU MUST CHOOSE!

For the rest of your life, would you... limit your clothing to various matador outfits for $350,000? $700,000?

YOU MUST CHOOSE!

INACTION

Would you... arm-wrestle the person to your right if the winner gets a dollar?

Would you... race the person to your left if the winner gets a dollar?

Would you... see who can do the best impersonation of President Obama among your friends if the winner gets a dollar?

Disclaimer: These questions are purely hypothetical (look it up.)
As responsible authors, we must insist on no wagering.
As such, contests should be for fun only.

YOU MUST CHOOSE!

Would you... pay a $300 service fee to have your doorbell changed to Darth Vader's Imperial March? What about any other song? What song would you pick?

YOU MUST CHOOSE!

For $100,000 deposited in your bank account today, which of the following would you give up for life?

Meat

Soap

Brushing your hair

Cutting your hair

Cutting your nails

Pronouns

YOU MUST CHOOSE!

CHAPTER ELEVEN

11

SUPER-SUPREMELY STRANGE

WOULD YOU RATHER.... HAVE YOUR HAIR GELLED FORWARD LIKE A BASEBALL HAT BRIM

OR GELLED UP IN A SPIKE LIKE A UNICORN HORN?

Would you rather...

snore loudly when you're awake

OR

always have your eyelids flipped up?

Would you rather...

when suntanning, wear a mesh shirt

OR

suspenders?

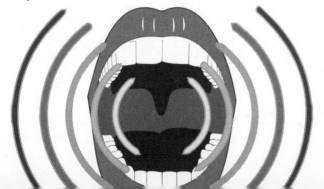

YOU MUST CHOOSE!

195

Would you rather...

change your first name to what it spells backwards (for example, Fred = Derf)

OR

your last name (for example, Jones = Senoj)?

Things to consider: Olive, Iris, Aidan, Bob, Anna

Accidental Education: A word or phrase that is spelled the same way forward and backwards is called a "palindrome." Palindromes include: "mom," "dad," "kayak," "race car," "Never odd or even," and "Go hang a salami! I'm a lasagna hog."

YOU MUST CHOOSE!

Would you rather...

stop aging at 20 **OR** at 30?

10 **OR** 50?

3 **OR** 60?

YOU MUST CHOOSE!

WEATHER OR NOT (GET IT?)

Would you rather...

have the weather in your room feel like the Amazon rainforest

OR

like the North Pole?

Things to consider: heavy blankets, night sweats, bugs

YOU MUST CHOOSE!

Would you rather...

feel like you're constantly in the middle of an earthquake

OR

on the fringe of a tornado?

Would you rather...

get caught in sloppy joe quicksand

OR

a trail mix hailstorm?

YOU MUST CHOOSE!

Would you rather...

have a baseball batting helmet permanently screwed to your head

OR

a baseball glove permanently sewn over your hand?

Would you rather...

suck on a hermit crab gobstopper

OR

snailcicle?

YOU MUST CHOOSE!

Would you rather...

never be able to face the person you are talking to

OR

feel a major shock any time you touch someone?

Things to consider: handshakes/meeting people, high-fives

YOU MUST CHOOSE!

Would you rather watch an action movie set in...

a cruise ship **OR** a 747?

Staples **OR** Michaels?

a doorknob store **OR** vacuum repair shop?

YOU MUST CHOOSE!

WOULD YOU RATHER...ONLY BE ABLE TO KEEP ONE EYE OPEN AT A TIME

OR ONLY BE ABLE TO KEEP ONE FOOT ON THE FLOOR AT A TIME?

Would you rather...

lose all your teeth one by one throughout the day (they grow back at night)

OR

lose all your hair throughout the night (it grows back gradually during the day)?

YOU MUST CHOOSE!

FARTS!

Would you rather...

perpetually smell farts **OR** perpetually smell *like* farts?

fart silently often **OR** loudly occasionally?

fart to the rhythm of the "Cups Song" intro **OR** be propelled upward in the air a few feet when you fart?

pass out after you fart **OR** suddenly become humorless and find all fart jokes offensive?

YOU MUST CHOOSE!

Would you rather...

have your worst secrets show up when people Google you

OR

have negative political commercial-type TV ads continuously running, smearing your reputation?

YOU MUST CHOOSE!

Would you rather...

when sick, only be able to throw up in mailboxes

OR

in mail slots?

YOU MUST CHOOSE!

THE AFTERLIFE

Would you rather...

be buried in you room with all your possessions like the Egyptian kings

OR

have your ashes scattered wherever you choose?

Follow up: What would you be buried with? Where would your ashes go?

YOU MUST CHOOSE!

When you get to heaven would you rather...

as an angel, have a waterbed cloud

OR

a regenerating funnel cake halo?

If sent to the Underworld, would you rather...

be sentenced to an eternity of untangling iPhone ear bud cords

OR

solving word problems?

YOU MUST CHOOSE!

WOULD YOU RATHER....LIVE IN A HOUSE DESIGNED BY DR. SEUSS

OR PLAY AN INSTRUMENT DESIGNED BY DR. SEUSS?

HONK!

Would you rather...

never forget a phone number **OR** a birthday?

never be able to say "please" **OR** "thank you?"

never again be able to use a toothbrush **OR** a towel?

YOU MUST CHOOSE!

Check out
WOULDYOURATHER.COM
for more
questions and fun!

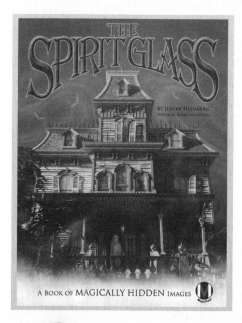